Breaking the Silence

J. Leonhart

Breaking the Silence

ISBN:1519517602
ISBN-13:9781519517609

To Jace

Breaking the Silence

CONTENTS

Breaking the Silence

ACKNOWLEDGMENTS

Thank you to Shonel, who dealt with my crazy ass sitting next to her for a year. She read this publication and gave me a lot of great feedback and even a little life advice that I'll carry with me for the rest of my life. She's underestimated by her peers way too often, she is amazing and I hope we stay friends for a while.

Thank you to my family. I haven't been able to thank them enough over the years, but without them I would be nothing.

Thank you to Trish, she testified as a character witness and held me when I cried. She's done so much for my family that I could never repay.

Thank you to the United States Air Force, specifically my leadership. You've been my second family. We've laughed and cried together, you saved my life, and you helped me get stronger.

Thank you to Finding Our Voices, you've been my sounding board and the surrogate for my advocacy. I am thankful for all of you lovely ladies that I've met and been to weekly group with. I appreciate you listening to my ramblings and for picking me back up when I fall off of the wagon.

And thank you for reading this, maybe you'll find something from my story. Obviously it isn't over, but I hope that you'll find hope and strength with whatever you do. Thank you again.

J. Leonhart

Introduction

I'm sure that other people are more qualified and talented to do this for me. I could sit in a comfy chair and just talk about my life as though it were of any importance to the world, while someone much younger than me eagerly writes down my experiences. Each word, each syllable being lapped up with the greatest pleasure and excitement. Sometimes I wish I were famous and that someone would want to write my epic memoirs, depicting me as some great heroine similar to Joan of Arc. I wish I could tell you a story that is about a brave, womanly warrior who fights her way to the freedom she so craves; that this warrior fights dragons and armies of trolls. I want to write you epic fight scenes that delve into the gore and heroics of the warrior and her faithful companions. That isn't going to happen, instead I will tell you a story about a little girl who grows up with terrible people, and how she becomes an ordinary "adult" (I use the term loosely) and manages to kind of get over her past and get to be a better person.

I've heard so many stories of other women and even men, who have had to experience horrific things in their lives. And they all have that one person that doesn't understand what PTSD or even depression is, and they don't care to comprehend how abuse affects every aspect of your being. There are a lot of stigmas about PTSD and depression. I've been told that I couldn't possibly have PTSD because I've never been in combat, that I've never seen a buddy get blown up down range. It's been assumed (by admittedly me more than anyone else) that I must be a weaker person because I developed PTSD and depression. That I need to just move on and get over it. Wrong. All of it wrong. I've experienced something that most people have only seen on crime shows, something that strangers, or even friends, cannot truly understand about me. Most people can't fathom that sexual assault happens outside of the seedy parts of town and only by strangers or when you drink. According to the RAINN (Rape, Abuse and Incest National Network), there are about 293,000 victims each year. But you don't see things like that on the news, they don't teach you about rape prevention in school.

I haven't seen a book that's written about sexual assault, about the person's overall experiences, like a survivor guide for dummies if you will… I know that I'm not a hero or a role model for survivors. I'm just getting by and still struggling just like everyone else. I don't have any secrets to how I've gotten through my experiences; I still have questions just like everyone else. I don't believe others when they tell me I'm strong, I believe that I've just been in the right place at the right time. I've had people around me that care, I've had a job that didn't discriminate against me and actually saved my life. I chalk all of my progress up to my reliance on my military leadership and the friends that I've made over the years.

But here it is, everything about my life that I know I haven't completed at the ripe age of 22, but it's time that someone broke the silence, I won't keep quiet anymore.

Off I Went Into the Wild Blue Yonder

In November of 2011, I shipped off to basic training for the United States Air Force. Most have asked why I joined, and I answer simply that I am a patriot and wanted to serve my country; I'm sad to say that isn't the only reason. I joined because I wanted to get away, I hated the situation I was in and I didn't feel confident enough to get into college. I learned a lot being an eighteen year old in a big Air Force world. Basic training wasn't too difficult for me, I had been yelled at for most of my life so having someone with a wide brimmed hat screaming at me didn't make a difference. Graduating basic training and technical training school had been the best accomplishments of my life, but my mother only came to see me graduate basic. She didn't seem too enthusiastic about the pride I had for my country. I kept dreaming that I would be some big shot senior non-commissioned officer, with so many people looking up to me for advice and guidance. I kept my secret to myself, I never sought out help for anything and let my feelings stay bottled up on the inside of my being. Until those feelings couldn't be contained anymore.

The Air Force saved my life. I don't mean that lightly, the leadership that I have had over the past 4 years of my Air Force career have saved my life both metaphorically and literally. My leadership took my hand and walked with me every step of the way, even past the trial. They have cried and cheered with me; they learned and made mistakes with me. I had found a family to take care of me while I was away from home. Not everyone is as lucky as I am to have had that much support.

My commanders called me weekly and even sent me cards while I was hospitalized, just to make sure that I was okay. My supervisors were concerned enough about my quality of life that they would frequently make sure that I wasn't having suicidal thoughts or thoughts of self-harming. They stayed patient with me when I felt I was out of control. I feel so grateful for having the experience that I've had with the military.

I know that not everyone has had the same experience with military life. I wake up before the sun every day to get to work on time, and in the winter I don't get home until the sun sets sometimes. I don't get to choose a lot about my life, like my hair and nails. Those things are trivial to me; I find comfort in the fact that I have a steady job that provides me and my cats with food and warmth. I don't regret joining the military whatsoever.

At times it is hard; I believe that the Air Force has provided me with an excuse to ignore my social issues. At the end of every day, I count my lucky stars for the people I've met that accepted me. I know that my leadership went through the ups and downs of prosecution with me, with meeting my biological father for the first time, with therapy and all of the day-to-day drama that I experience in my anxiety-filled mind. I would name every person but unfortunately that would take up this entire book. And whether or not I decide to stay in the military or eventually let my time end, I'd like to still serve my country by helping others like myself. Hopefully that dream comes true.

Clammy Hands

My hands have always been clammy. My mother used to point it out very deliberately to me when I was growing up, she told me that it was the reason why she didn't want to hold my hand. But little girls need mothers to hold their hands when they're learning to walk, otherwise they don't know how to take the right steps. My mother was always a very critical person; I spent my time trying to please her. I wore the clothes she wanted me to wear; I tried being athletic and artistic, I tried to be the smartest in my classes so that she would be proud of me. You can't be proud of a child you don't love. I remember desperately wanting something for us to do together. I tried scrapbooking, I became a really avid reader, and I started loving football just to be around her as much as I could. Nothing worked. We needed to bond over something since I was her only daughter, but she never tried. My mother had no desire to bond with me at all. I think she preferred to manipulate what I saw in the mirror.

My mother wasn't an abused child; she grew up with loving and nurturing parents. My mother had so much love surrounding her, her step-sister and half-sister loved her dearly. My mother went to a small high school in Oklahoma, but she didn't lack friends or after-school activities. She was a track star, and she was beautiful. I loved looking at her pictures in the den of my grandmother's house when I was little; she was a gorgeous and amazingly smart woman. I wanted to be pretty like her, I wanted all of the freckles she had and the big curly hair. I always wanted her handwriting, as silly as that sounds; her penmanship was beautiful and I've always envied it. I once took a page out of her notebook and tried to trace over the letters so I could train my hands to write like hers. I loved the way that she watched Jeopardy!, she could answer almost all of the questions, even when she was mad at me I would peek my head from behind the couch so that I could watch with her. I loved the way she watched Young and the Restless, she recorded every episode and watched them as soon as she got home from work, and she reacted to all of the plot twists and made the characters' facial responses as she watched. I don't think my mother ever believed me when I told her that I loved her, and how excited I was when she wanted to go to band booster club meetings and to the places where I performed. I wanted her to watch me do the things that I loved; I wanted her to be proud of the fact that I was good at those things. I followed her around blindly, and I believed everything that she told me. But I was invisible to her. I've always been afraid of disappointing her, and it seemed like I could never impress her enough to notice anything I did.

Have you ever seen a painting burn? It's so

pretty before, and then the paint starts to bubble and the canvas curls and turns brown from the heat. That's exactly what happened to my childhood image of my mother. After she had completely taken my offender's side during His prosecution, she told me how much she hated me. I found out that she had lied about my biological father, and told me that he never wanted me anyway. She blamed me for everything that went wrong in her life, like it wasn't her choice to have unprotected sex. I don't think that she ever noticed the scars on my cheek; she didn't even know she left them. I always believed that children were supposed to get punished physically by their mothers; she told me that it built character. I obeyed the strict curfews and never questioned the things they didn't teach me, I didn't pry when my questions about life situations went unanswered. I kept my darkest secret from her until I finally left home.

I don't know what I could've possibly done to make her hate me. I don't know how a mother could testify against her daughter in a court of law to protect her pedophile husband. But there are a lot of things that I will never comprehend. Mothers are supposed to be protectors and love their children unconditionally; at least that's what I see in other mothers, so I've never understood what happened to mine. I'm afraid of her, I'm afraid that she's going to hurt the ones that I love, and I'm afraid that she will keep my brother away from me forever. I tremble at the thought of ever running into her.

He Is NOT the Father

As much as I'd love to fill this entire chapter with reasons why I hate my abuser, I know that I shouldn't. I know that no one could ever believe that Hitler enjoyed architecture or listening to music, but the cold hard truth is that people aren't horrible 24 hours a day, 365 days a year. There's a lot of my personality that I got from my abuser, he taught me things that I still use today and hobbies that I still love.

My abuser was born to a strict Italian mother and her G.I. husband; they met in

Belgium and married, conceived, and birthed there. They moved back to Texas, where His father was from, and His mother became an American citizen. His parents are really strict Catholics; they go to church every Sunday and have the stereotypical views on modern society. They always treated me like an outsider, so I wasn't surprised when I found out why they hated me, it made me realize that they hated me because of my mother's mistakes rather than my personality.

While my mother made me believe that she and my abuser met while He was active duty army, and conceived me before He went overseas to Germany for 2 years. He came back, they married, and I was the flower girl at their wedding. I know that you're hoping that the story is true, happiness and all that jazz... However, it is one of the biggest, fattest lies that my mother ever told. I was another man's child, one who she apparently didn't want in her life or mine. She lied about the biological beginnings of my life, only to reveal, after her precious husband was charged with incest, that He was "NOT THE FATHER"; as though we were on Jerry Springer.

My abuser wasn't always horrible, we went fishing and I liked going to the lake with him to touch the slimy fish scales and have the satisfaction of catching one by myself. We watched Star Wars together and we made light sabers out of empty paper towel rolls to battle each other in the living room while we watched it. He got me into all of the superheroes, I've always liked Aquaman the best, and he would tell me their stories and we watched action movies together. He could draw and paint very well; I wanted to be an artist like him. I liked to watch all of the gory movies that my mother didn't like me to watch, he always let me get away with things. When my brother was born, I felt forgotten. I got older and my mother yelled at me more. I wasn't good enough, I wasn't pretty enough, I wasn't smart enough. I had to protect my brother now so that he wouldn't get swept under the rug with me.

My abuser protected me a lot, and told me to buck up and not listen to my mother's criticisms. That protection came with a horrifying price, one that I didn't know I didn't have to pay. He promised that he would keep her at bay, that he would protect me from her. Every time she was mad at me for something, he would come into my room to get His payment. He always apologized the next day. He would take me to lunch or let me watch a movie in the living room. So I thought that he knew he was wrong, and he always promised that it was the last time. It kept progressing and it got a lot worse with time. He would always ask me to stay home to do chores, but I never got the chance to get them done, so I would get yelled at by my mother for not doing them. This is how my life was for almost 3 years. I was afraid of the darkness; I slept with sweatpants and a sweatshirt on for protection, even in the summer. I was afraid of hearing muffled footsteps, and of creaking doors. I was afraid of being home alone by myself. I'm still afraid of all of those things. I couldn't escape, I could never fight back. No one could hear my muffled screaming, and if someone did, then no one wanted to help me. I felt so alone, and crying about it made it worse. He told me that no one would ever believe me.

The worst experience I ever had, happened when I was 16; my abuser had told me that He wanted me on His own bed. He made me lay there on my mother's side of the bed as He groped me. He put her pillow over my face, it smelled like coconuts and vanilla. This was the bed that my mother slept in, that my brother crawled into at night when he had a bad dream. I was sobbing from shame and guilt. He put a towel over me gingerly, like He was protecting me from himself. He left for only a second as He went to his closet gun safe and grabbed his glock. I didn't know if it was loaded, I just heard the click of the safety being shut off and him checking the chamber. He held the gun out to me and told me that if I killed myself first he would follow right after. He even had put the gun in my hand, it was cold and stiff. It felt like a final decision. I imagined what it would feel like to shoot myself for a brief moment, and if anyone would even miss me. When I told him no, he called me a coward. He told me that I was pathetic and disgusting. He hit me and left me crying in the living room, wishing that I had taken that gun and shot myself, just to get it all over with.

What hurt the most about the whole

situation was that I trusted him. He was supposed to protect me, but instead was one of the worst people in my life. And He made me feel like I was crazy, like I had no idea what I was talking about and that I had just made the whole thing up. He never apologized. Never looked at me. He didn't even speak for himself at his trial. Complete silence. At least He could've been a decent person and admitted to what he had done, but you can't trust a convicted sex offender.

OFF WITH HIS HEAD!

I didn't know what sexual assault actually was until I joined the military. They don't teach you those things in school. I think that schools just expect your parents to teach you those things, but I guess no one really realizes how often it happens in the home. I didn't know that my father wasn't supposed to teach me about physical love. I didn't know that it's illegal for your father to threaten your life or lay sweating on top of you early in the morning. I felt like no one would ever believe me, like I would have to carry this burden for the rest of my life. I felt broken, and disgusting, I started to think that I actually was making it up; that I was just having terrible nightmares every night. But I wasn't. I had too many real memories of what was going on, even though most of the time it was just pieces of what had happened. I was terrified of my grandfather; I thought all men did that to little girls. I locked myself in my room whenever he was the only one home. Even looking back now, I'm horrified how afraid I was of the man that had been one of the only good male influences in my life.

I spent my first few months in the military trying to distract myself from my home life. I went hiking and tried to do all of the things that nineteen year olds do. I kept to myself most of the time at work; I envied all of the others that didn't wake up in the middle of the night with sweat-filled sheets because of a nightmare. I was terrified to sleep without a light on and a knife next to my bed. My appendix burst in August of 2012, and I had a lot of trouble staying out of the hospital after that. I went to the ER with severe stomach pains one day; my supervisor drove me from work. I guess in a morphine-induced stupor, I asked my supervisor if she wanted to have children someday. I began telling her about how I would get an abortion if I ever got unexpectedly pregnant, because I wouldn't want to bring a child in to such a painful world. I told her about how my mother hated me and how I wished I was dead. I divulged the secrets that I hadn't told a single soul until that moment. I felt like I couldn't stop my mouth from spilling all of the words I had kept hidden from the world for so long. I knew that she had gotten scared for me; I was in the worst of emotional places at the time. I hope now that she doesn't hate me for the things she had to hear later on in that year.

Just before Thanksgiving in 2012, I was faced with having my gall bladder removed due to developing gall stones, I was stressed enough with the things that I had told my supervisor. She was the first person that listened to me and didn't judge me for the things I felt. I knew that my abuser was coming to where I was stationed for the holiday; he told me he wanted to relive old memories with me. It finally gave me enough fear to tell someone; I didn't think that I could have the strength to fight him. I never did anyway. I didn't know that my supervisor was mandated to report a sexual assault if her subordinate told her about it, but I didn't know where else to go for help. I was thrust into the criminal justice system without even thinking about whether or not I would ever want to press charges against him. I found myself sitting in the SARC office on base, and then with OSI agents who made me recall as much painfully horrifying details that I could. The officers conference called the Plano Police Department and I had to tell my story all over again to someone I wouldn't meet until the trial. I had to go to mental health and see a therapist, who had to listen to my story too. I was embarrassed that I was pulled out of work in front of everyone just to talk about my offender.

He was arrested a couple days before Christmas of 2012; his parents went to Texas and bailed him out of jail. He got a lawyer, apparently a family lawyer because they had worked with him before. I went home despite the fact that my mother and offender were there, I wanted to be with my grandparents. It was in my room, in the middle of an episode of America's Next Top

Model I might add, that I found out that he wasn't my biological father; that my mother was even more irresponsible than I had originally thought. My mother had asked my grandparents to never say anything to me; she wanted it to be her little secret that she would take to her grave. I only found out because she had told her lawyer to get lesser charges for her beloved. I was so confused; I was hurt that my entire family had kept such a huge secret from me. I wanted to feel nothing, I wanted to make horrible decisions and I wanted to die. How could anything possibly get any worse? But it was only the beginning.

I began to deteriorate once the New Year started; I purposefully failed inspections because I wanted to get kicked out of the military. I knew I couldn't do anything stupid like drunk driving or drug using, I didn't even know how to get drugs and I hardly ever left base to drunk drive or even get alcohol. I didn't want to go to jail so going AWOL wasn't an option. I wanted to kill myself and not have the Air Force know, I didn't want to make anyone go out of their way for me. I was tired of everyone lying to me, and I was tired of being another statistic and being a burden to my broken family. But my leadership and my therapist wouldn't have it. So in May of 2013, I was sent to check into a psychiatric hospital.

My 28-day stay was not pleasant in the slightest, I hated that I was immersed in my trauma. I hated that meals were specified times and that I couldn't just walk outside whenever I wanted. I hated that I had to check-out my razor and hair dryer to get dressed in the morning. I hated that I couldn't have my phone for most of the day. I felt pressured to cry and feel things that I was incapable of feeling, I didn't feel sorry for myself and I didn't gain anything from my stay in the hospital. I only enjoyed the people that I met and the outside activities that we got to do. I met women that were amazing. We passed notes during group and laughed at funny movies that the group decided to watch. I regret that I don't keep in touch with them anymore.

The months leading up to the trial were excruciating. It kept being pushed back because the defendant couldn't pay for his lawyer. I spent Christmas of 2013 with good friends, because I was too scared to go home. I went to Texas on

February 1st to face my offender for the last time, but I didn't know that at the time obviously. I went to the first day of the trial in my service dress. I was so nervous. They questioned his witnesses first, my mother, my brother, my mother's friend, and his friend. The only defense they had was about a knife that they tried to say he bought for me; my best friend confirmed that it was bought in the state of Colorado. Another was a picture of me after tech school, he wasn't there but the defense claimed that he was in the reflection of my sunglasses in the picture; which was also untrue, and more than far-fetched. I waited for days in a room with my family watching MTV and other daytime shows. Then came my time to testify, I was the second to last person. The last person to testify was a licensed psychiatrist who specialized in PTSD. I took my Airman's coin with me because I couldn't keep my hands still. I saw his face and I froze. My entire body went cold, it was the first time I had seen him in almost 3 years. His parents sat behind him with a small boy with them, I hated seeing the look on that poor boy's face when I had to go into detail about what had happened to me. I asked for just my Aunt to be in the room with me, there are a lot of things that my grandparents don't know about my assault, I prefer to keep it that way. I wanted someone to look at to give me strength, I know it killed her inside, I could see it in her eyes. She never told me anything about how she felt during my testimony. I would intermittently look at the jury, most of them couldn't hide their surprise or any of their other emotions, and it made me feel even more embarrassed. My offender's parents gave me death stares the entire time I was on the stand, like I was the one on trial and not their beloved son. I hated that they still stood by him, I hated that my mother sat on the other side of the large wooden door that I stared at from the stand. My hands got clammy; I knew I was sweating through my layers of uniform. I felt embarrassed to be in uniform and testifying about being raped. I didn't want the jury to think differently of me, I wished that I didn't have to have my chair facing him, but it couldn't have been helped. This hell went on for a week; they apparently went through my school records and notes from counselors. Apparently people noticed how different I was back then, but no one decided to say anything.

When all of the witnesses had been questioned, it was time for the jury to decide whether or not he was guilty. He was charged with four counts of aggravated sexual assault of a child, four counts of indecency with child sexual contact, and five counts of aggravated sexual assault. The judge read all of the charges, my face got hot and my grandmothers held my hands tighter with each charge. They didn't know about a lot of the charges or what actually had happened, but they never asked me for details. He was convicted of 6 out of those 13 charges. I held my breath, it all felt surreal. My mother screamed, and his mother burst into tears. I ran out of the courtroom and fell to the floor outside, I burst into tears. It's a moment that I will always remember. I had won, people believed me. He wouldn't hurt anyone anymore, he couldn't do anything. My family surrounded me, all crying our eyes out. I regret not being able to see him handcuffed and taken into custody to wait for his sentencing. But when we all finally got home, I slept the best that I had in years. I felt safe.

We came in early the next day for sentencing. I spent most of the drive there trying to figure out what I was going to say to my offender before the jury decided his fate. I kept it simple; I honestly don't remember what I said. But I know that it was to the extent of telling him how I will never forgive him for the pain that he put me and my family through, and that I hope he spends his life thinking about what he had done and how I was the one that stood up and said something rather than cowering for the rest of my life....something like that. After I spoke, we went back to the dreaded TV room to wait, once again, for the jury to decide what kind of sentence he would get. My lawyer pulled me aside at this point and asked me if I wanted to do a plea bargain; for those who have no idea what I'm talking about, this is when the prosecution and the defense agree on an allotted sentence that's mutually beneficial. In my case, this was 35 years without an appeal, as in he wouldn't try to fight his sentence and he would just sit in jail and then after 17 years he would be up for parole. But, in the state of Texas, not very many convicted sex offenders get parole the first time, so it was explained that there was a 98% chance that he would be sitting in jail for 35 years; which was twice the amount of time that he spent torturing me in my home. I agreed, simply because I never wanted to control someone's life that way. I just wanted to be believed. I wanted him to be exposed as the monster he was, not keep him in a box forever until he died. The jury had sentenced him for 6 life sentences when we finally went back into the courtroom, but my lawyer explained the bargain and he was handcuffed shortly thereafter. I watched as my mother hugged and kissed him, and as my brother started crying. I stood and watched because I wanted them to know that I was there, that I was always going to be there regardless of what they tried to do to me. I wanted to see the defeat in his eyes before he was sent out of my life forever. I'll never forget the look he had on his face before he was locked up for the next 35 years.

He was sent to a prison in south Texas, one that is known to be one of the toughest facilities. I don't expect him to be a celebrated felon, assaulting a child is disgusting to even the nastiest of murderers or drug dealers. I won't ever have to see him again, but sometimes I wish that I had at least gotten an apology; one where I could see the sincerity or at least some remorse for what he had done. The press wrote an article about it in the Dallas Morning News, they tried to protect my identity, but I was the only female from my graduating class to join the military. And obviously we shared a last name. Comments started popping up after a couple of weeks, but it wasn't anything that made me upset. I honestly wasn't bothered by it, his picture sits in the top right corner of the article online; sometimes, I look at it, just to remind myself of what I had accomplished. I obviously felt guilty at first, but I realized that I had taken one bad person out of society. And I'm proud of myself for that.

SURVIVING

I wasn't in the best shape after the trial, his family started sending me threats via Facebook and my mother wouldn't even answer my emails. I was a little discouraged that the two people I wanted in my life wouldn't have anything to do with me. I became obsessed with what they were doing and tried so hard to get them to talk to me, I even tried a fake Instagram account to talk to my brother. But they had both been brainwashed, they both told me how terrible I was, and how I took the only person that loved them away.

Everyone keeps telling me to wait, that one day my brother will come around and realize all of the lies that he's been told. I'm not going to hold my breath for that to happen, but my mother, she is someone that I don't care for anymore. She has lied too many times to count, and she scorned her only daughter. She has never been a good mother, so she can't be mine anymore.

When I was little, I asked God to make it all stop, to make my mother love me, to tell me what to do to make my dad stop touching me. I prayed silently every night when I heard the muffled carpet footsteps from across the apartment. I told God that I would never ever do anything bad again, that I would become a nun and devote myself to Him. I hadn't been to church since I was twelve and I prayed to nothing. It never stopped, it never went away, and I never forgot it.

I guess in the end, I would do absolutely anything to have my memories erased.

After the trial, I changed my name, He wasn't my real father and I didn't want his name plastered to my being. It was like my prison chain that I finally cut loose. For about the next 6 months, I never told a soul about my abuse. I refused to have a victim advocate and I tried to hide my face every time I went to mental health. I was ashamed of being a survivor. I didn't want to be a statistic of a horrible crime. I kept so many of my own secrets that I started to go stir crazy; I was being this person that I didn't want to be. I was around all of these fake and terrible people that didn't care about me or my accomplishments. My vision of the world was clouded because I didn't know who I was and who I wanted to be. I scurried through my life making sure to stay in the shadows. I started to write about how dark figures following me and how it felt like no one could save me. I was plagued by my abuse, and how even though it seemed as though I had won, it felt like I was dealing with the consequences of someone else's mistakes. I knew that people viewed me as broken, that men saw me as damaged goods; and I was, I let myself feel that way and it kept me from being who I wanted. I cared too much about what others thought of me and how I wanted to been seen. I was the only one of my kind and I hated it. I felt like no one understood the daily struggles that I had. But I also didn't want to be seen as abnormal. Finding out that I wasn't the only human in the entire world that had been raped was the most comforting feeling, because I didn't feel as strange and unnatural.

I stumbled this way until February of 2015; this was when I first met Joyce. On February 9th, I had gone to my weekly therapy appointment, I told my therapist how alone I felt, and how I wanted to make a difference in the world. He handed me a newspaper clipping for a support group called Finding Our Voices.

Finding My Voice

Finding Our Voices is an excellent group. I have met so many amazing people and learned so much about myself and the world that I never could without the support group every week. Before my therapist gave me the newspaper clipping about the organization, I didn't know what my purpose was; I was self-conscious, lonely, and severely depressed. I was afraid of the world and what it thought about me and my past, at the time I felt like just a statistic and I didn't feel like putting my offender in prison actually did anything for me. I felt more guilt than I had before, and I honestly did not have the passion and hunger for anything in my life. When I first learned about this organization, I was a little hesitant about going. I thought that no one would understand me or the things I had gone through. I thought that it would be like an Alcoholics Anonymous meeting where I would have to begin every meeting with "My name is Jacobi and I'm a victim of sexual assault." I didn't want to be labeled by the crime someone else had committed; I didn't want to be defined by something so terrible. I forced myself to go to that first meeting; I was the only one that had been there that first night with Ms. Joyce. Ironically, it was the one year anniversary of putting my offender away. I tried not to give away too much of my life, and I was afraid that she wouldn't accept me. But once she started talking, she changed my life. She revealed that she was a survivor too, that our stories weren't that different. She made me feel safe, not only physically, but emotionally as well. I started going every Tuesday after that, meeting more amazing women and learning about how they deal with their lives. It gave me something to look forward to every week instead of isolating myself in my apartment. I started to become much more confident with Joyce around; I began showing more of my personality at group than I ever did at work or at home. The art show was a very pivotal point in my life, I was so afraid of reading my poetry and telling a bunch of strangers about my life. But Joyce gives me so much courage; she all but held my hand onto the makeshift stage to tell my story. That day was the first day I had ever cried in front of anyone but my family. After looking into the faces of the audience and the other survivors sitting next to me, I found my calling. I decided that this was what I wanted to do; I wanted to help sexual assault survivors. I wanted to be a Sexual Assault Response Coordinator for the military, I wanted to advocate and educate the world about this heinous crime. I wanted to show other survivors that they could have courage and stand tall against the stereotypes and the victim blaming and anything else life and society threw at them. Finding Our Voices showed me all of this; it helped me realize my purpose that I don't think the universe had intended for me. I stand a bit taller after every single meeting I attend. My family, friends, and co-workers have all seen the difference that FOV helped me make. I'm not afraid anymore, because of how amazing Finding Our Voices has been to me.

ANGER: THE #@*&%^ STAGE

I've been seeing a therapist weekly since 2012, and I feel like I've gotten to the point in my healing where I'm just straight up angry. I'm mad at my mother for not being a mother to me, I'm mad at my offender for being so stupid and ruining the lives of my family. I'm mad at His family, because they all think I'm some sort of monster that has done nothing but crap on their lives. It frustrates me that there are people who don't believe me and they think I would have a legitimate reason to lie and put someone in jail.

(Because OBVIOUSLY I did that for giggles) I had so much more to lose, I had my reputation, my freedom, my job, everything. Why on earth would I lie about that?

Sometimes I still have days where I'm empty inside, and others I feel like a bad ass ready to take on any villain. I don't think that I'm necessarily done with my hardships; I'll always have good days and bad days despite being "fully healed" or not. Unfortunately, I will always live with the consequences of my abusers decisions. While he sits in jail, I have flashbacks, and anxiety, and fear. I get treated differently by others because being a survivor of sexual assault equates to some infectious disease that no one wants to catch. My life has been put on display even though I was not the accused, and I hate that I face more punishment than he ever will. I've been a lot more open about my experiences (quite obviously), mostly because I wouldn't wish this emotional, mental, and physical pain on anyone.

I've tried to immerse myself into the issue of victim advocacy; I want to be the voice for so many that can't find theirs yet. I want to be the strong voice for everyone. Sometimes this tends to exhaust me, and I get a little discouraged when I can't change something, but I think that in the end it would be worth it to change someone's life for the better. There is so much information on how to not be a victim, but nothing about not being a perpetrator or how to deal with it afterwards. I went in blindly with nothing but the people around me as bumpers to keep me from falling into the darkest parts of my depression.

In April of 2015, I decided that it was time to be a part of the solution rather than hiding behind a mask. April is national sexual assault awareness month, and every Friday the base wore teal. I worked a booth at the Base Exchange to give out free goodies for passers-by. Every month my base had something called Wing Warfit, where the entire base got together and did fitness training together, now on this month the SARC asked me to speak in front of everyone and thank them for supporting me with their awareness and participation. This meant that I was essentially outing myself to the entire base, being a previous officer of one of the biggest organizations on base, I was terrified. I saw so many familiar faces in the crowd, and I felt crazy for even agreeing to do that. I'm pretty sure that I blacked out from the anxiety, but after I ran away with my vision going blurry, the SARC told me that she saw other survivors in the crowd that were in awe of me, and some even approached her about me saying that I was incredibly brave and I was an example for them. It was that moment that I decided what I wanted to do with my life. I wanted to show others like me that it was okay to speak out, that there are so many people that care about them than they realize. I wanted to help the military and the civilian community to understand what it's like to be a survivor. I decided that I wanted to be a SARC; I wanted to go to school for social work and be the person that Joyce was for me. I'm so incredibly lucky to have had the criminal justice experience that I've had. I had leadership that called me every weekend while I was at Haven Behavioral hospital for PTSD to make sure that I was okay and they even asked me about my therapy. But I know that others haven't had the support that I have, it breaks my heart to meet people that don't have the resources to get therapy, or to even get out of their situation. I want to be a part of many happily ever afters and I want others to have the support they need the most.

No one tells you that you'll always have a small emptiness in your heart where trust and love used to be. I've had to learn the hard way that there isn't anything I can do to fill the void that my mother left when I last heard her voice in December of 2012. I can't fix all of my family like I want to, but they're broken just like my heart and my spirit. Sex offenders don't treat their victims with care, they batter them around and break them with ease, but they don't stay around to pick up the pieces to put these people back together. I've learned that sexual assault doesn't just affect one individual; it affects their families, and the people that they meet. I know that I will never be an entire person; I tattooed the teal ribbon for sexual assault prevention behind my left shoulder to signify the pain that I'll always have behind me. It's a reminder of why I want to do the things that I do for others, to help other survivors get through their hard times and to get rid of rape all together.

LETTERS TO THE EDITORS OF MY LIFE

Dearest Mother,

I apologize for being the scum of the earth; I know that I am the sum of every possible bad thing you could think of. Cancer + Hitler + Racism+ Famine + War = Me. I get it. I really do....but I really think that you're just looking at your image instead of mine. I've lived most of my life trying to please you, to make you notice me as your daughter. I've accomplished so much in my short time on this earth and you've never acknowledged any of it. Mothers are supposed to unconditionally love their children; I don't understand what made you hate me despite my stay inside of your body for 9 months. How can you believe him over me? Why did you testify against me during his trial? I might not ever know, but it would be nice for you to at least acknowledge the fact that you're a bad parent. I wish that you would be put away too, or at least have my brother taken away from you. You're too narcissistic to care for another human being, and I hate that my brother has to grow up this way. And I know that you've told him that I'm not his real sister, but I grew up with him and loved him more like a mother than a sister. You've done nothing but lie to everyone around you, and take advantage of the kindness you've received. I'm sick of trying to please you; I'm tired of trying to reconnect with you; because you're not worth a second of my time. You had your chance to love me and treat me the way I deserve to be treated, like a human being, like your daughter.

Dear Asshole,

You've really messed up dude, like royally pissed off the wrong kinds of people. I don't know how you could possibly live with yourself; you unfortunately have time to think about all of the things you've done. You single-handedly ruined a handful of lives forever, including your son's. Your bad decisions have been like a domino effect, and I don't even think that you're remorseful. Did you enjoy hitting me and making me feel worthless? Was it all worth your freedom? I don't know why you got that sick satisfaction from hurting me like that, YOU are the worthless one. YOU are the disgusting one. You can't lie to me anymore, and you can't hurt me or anyone else ever again. Because of you, I've been psychiatrically hospitalized, alienated by my own mother, threatened by your shit family, and have had to deal with the eternal consequences for your actions. My family has suffered, my career has suffered, my mental status has suffered, and all because you were horny and wanted sexual gratification from a little girl. You're nothing to me anymore, I won't even say your name because I can't stand the way that it sounds. You're not my father, not even my step-father. You betrayed me in every single possible way that someone can be betrayed. You were my father, whether or not I was your biological child or even adopted child, you still had a responsibility to keep me safe and you failed miserably. You didn't care about anyone but yourself, and I'm glad that I'm not like you or my mother. I'm glad that I got the help that I needed so that I wouldn't ever have to be like you. And I hope and pray to every deity that my brother will never see you again, I don't want him to see you like that; because from the mugshot that I saw shortly after the trial, you look miserable and pathetic. I hear that Hell has pretty tropical weather, so I hope you're excited about where you're going.

I honestly don't know where I would be if it weren't for my grandparents. I grew up looking forward to seeing them during holidays; I liked listening to Pawpaw's stories about the planes he worked on and Grammy's adventures with their dogs Chance and Lil Bit. I cherished the letters that my Granddad sent me; I still have most of them. I re-read them sometimes and I don't know how he could ever come up with enough kid content for a 2-page letter, but it was really the crazy stickers that I looked forward to. I love the smell of my G.G., she always smells clean and warm, and it always reminds me of home and of watching TV with her, or sitting outside in their pool. My grandparents have all been my surrogate parents since I grew up with pretty terrible ones.

They stuck with me through the entire ordeal, and held me when I cried during the trial. I've tried to stay strong for them; because I know they all wished they had noticed something before so I could've avoided all of this pain. I think that everyone feels like that. But I know that they will always be by my side no matter what, and I feel comforted and blessed knowing that I'm not alone like most survivors. I'm so thankful for all of the things they've given and provided me that my mother didn't care about giving. I hate to think that they believe they are responsible for my mother's behavior, but I truly believe that she is mentally ill, or brainwashed to a point that she's still being controlled now that her husband is in jail. I think that she is afraid of what will happen once she takes responsibility for the terrible things she's done.

I feel responsible for the pain that they've gone through. My mother disowned her own parents, and won't let them see their only grandson. None of us will ever get to see him grow or help him into the right directions in life. We can only wait and wonder when he will finally come home and hold us again.

To My GG,

> I love you so much; you've been the mother that I never had. You pushed me to be the best person that I could be despite my horrible childhood. You held me when I cried, and you told me I was beautiful when my mother was telling me that I wasn't. I love calling you every day just to hear your voice; I appreciate your opinions about life and social situations. I hate that your daughter disowned you. I hate that she's been such a brat despite all of the things I know you've done for her. I know it's difficult to not have your child or your grandson, and I know that we just have to wait for my brother to come back to us. I hope you don't blame yourself, my life hasn't been your fault, it was my mother's choices that made me so

depressed and traumatized. Sometimes I wish that I didn't need to call you that I could just deal with things on my own, because sometimes I can hear the pain in your voice when you hear me crying over the phone. I know that it's been hard to be there for me when I'm so far away. But hopefully I'll be home soon, for good this time.

To My Granddad,

Thank you. You've been my rock through everything; you've taken care of the logistics so to speak. I'm sorry that you've had to deal with this, I'm sorry that you had to testify for me at trial. I'm sorry that you've had to deal with my crazy ass for the past 22 years and had to be my father when I didn't have one. I love you.

To My PawPaw,

I hope you don't blame yourself either, I know that this is specifically hard on you since my mother is your only biological child. But she isn't worth it; she is only trying to take advantage of your love. You are an amazing man and you shouldn't feel guilty for the behavior and rude actions of your daughter, she made her poor choices and now she has to live with them. I love you.

To My Grammy,

You didn't ask for any of this drama, but I'm so glad that you've been a solid fixture in my life. I know that there is a lot that you don't want to know, but you're supportive of me anyway. I love you and I hope to hang out with you and Benji, the puppy, sometime soon.

I have two happy places that I escape to when I'm scared or sad. In the first, I can feel the hot Texas sun on my face as I float in the pool in my GG and Granddad's backyard. My GG is sitting on a towel at the edge with her feet in the water and "singing" to Build Me Up Buttercup on the radio. She's wearing her wicker hat and one-piece bathing suit. My Granddad is scrubbing the sides of the pool because he can't ever relax. He starts to splash my GG and I giggle at the sound of her bubbling laughter. Perfection. My other happy place is on the land that my PawPaw used to own. My favorite thing to do was mow the yard; I loved the sound that it made. I wave at the horses I named Brownie and Blondie that live on the land next door. I wave to my Grammy who is standing on the porch with a small dog in each hand with a big grin on her face. When I'm done I go to the garage to watch my PawPaw work on his truck, he always smelled like motor oil and fresh cut grass. These are the places that I escape to.

To My Biological Father,

> I know that this whole mess was not what you wanted from a daughter that you never knew. I know that I've been pretty distant since we met, but I'm trying to figure my life out before I get to know you better. Right now, I'm struggling to find my place in this world and distance myself from the parent that didn't want me. I don't blame you for not being around, I know that my mother kept us apart and I'm sure that you're an amazing father. I'm

just scared of screwing up someone else and having another parent that hates me. It's difficult for me to accept that I'm not an unwanted child, and that I've finally found the parent that I've always dreamed of having.

To My Brother,

Despite what our mother might've told you, I AM your sister. I love you dearly and I hate that I can't talk to you about my day. I've tried so hard to keep you safe, but I don't think that I've succeeded. Everything that I've done has been to protect you; I just wanted you to be safe. I desperately hope that you read this to forgive me; I did what I had to. I didn't lie about anything; everything that has happened is in this book. The evidence is all outlined here. I hate that I've missed you grow up; Grammy told me that she saw pictures when mother visited them; she said that you were very tall and handsome. By the time you read this, you'll probably be taller than me! I hope that you're finding yourself amongst this mess, the last I heard you were in band playing the clarinet and I hoped that you followed in my nerdy footsteps. I know this will sound weird, but you sent me a school picture while I was in basic training, and I've kept that picture all of these years to remember what you looked like. I keep it in my favorite journal that I write poems in. It's a little battered, because I kept it in my ID holder during basic training and technical training school, but it sits in my most secret place so I can look at it and remember how it felt when you called me "sissy" for the first time or when you and I played Legos and G.I. Joes. I wish I could give you a hug, or watch you ride your bike again. You were my best friend for the longest time. I miss you and love you Bubba, and I hope to see you again someday.

My Soap Box

I was very lucky to have the experience that I had. Despite the pain that I was and continue to be in, I've been very supported by both the Air Force and my remaining family. But this is something that no one ever wants to talk about. I conduct trainings all of the time for the military as a Volunteer Victim Advocate, and no one ever joins the conversations that I seem to have with myself at the front of a large room of people. But why does it have to be so hard? As a survivor, I've had to tell so many people about my life and about my abuse. My life was put on blast for the world to see, so no one can tell me that they don't want to talk about it. It's time to talk about it; it's time to put away the "anti-rape" underwear, and the nail polish that detects date-rape drugs. I shouldn't have to learn karate to protect myself against rape. I don't necessarily think that everyone should walk down the street butt naked, but I should be able to go to a club and not be on my guard about men who creepily try to slip something into my drink. I shouldn't have to carry around small weapons just because some men and women can't control their sexual urges. I understand that it is my responsibility to stay safe, but I shouldn't be so afraid, no one should. Why are people pushing sex on other people? If an individual says that they don't want sex, and then don't force them; you wouldn't shove the scrapbook you painstakingly designed for a friend in their face asking them for their opinion of it, or force food down their throat because you wanted them to eat it. Be respectful, we all live in this crazy world together. Let's worry less about who people marry or what gender they want to be, let's fix a problem that has literally gone on for thousands of years so that we can move on and be a happier world. I'm willing to fix this and make the world safer. I know that we don't get a handbook on life or get a cheat sheet with all of the answers on the test. But the least that I can provide you is a way to see the subject of sexual assault from another perspective, from someone that has experienced it and is living with it. Sexual assault is something that everyone is embarrassed to talk about, but I'm here to tell you that it's time to start talking.